Great Historic Debates and Speeches™

THE FEDERALIST–ANTI-FEDERALIST DEBATE OVER STATES' RIGHTS

A PRIMARY ◄—► SOURCE ◄—► INVESTIGATION

Lea Ball

rosen central
Primary Source™
The Rosen Publishing Group, Inc., New York

Published in 2005 by The Rosen Publishing Group, Inc.
29 East 21st Street, New York, NY 10010

Copyright © 2005 by The Rosen Publishing Group, Inc.

First Edition

Library of Congress Cataloging-in-Publication Data

Ball, Lea.
The Federalist–Anti-Federalist debate over states' rights / by Lea Ball.—1st ed.
    p. cm.—(Great historic debates and speeches)
Includes bibliographical references (p.) and index.
ISBN 1-4042-0149-1 (lib. bdg.)
1. State rights—History—18th century—Juvenile literature. 2. Federal government—United States—History—18th century—Juvenile literature. 3. Federalist. 4. United States—Politics and government—1783–1789—Juvenile literature.
I. Title. II. Series.
JK316.B35 2004
320.473'049—dc22

2004001847

Manufactured in the United States of America

Cover images: Left: Portrait of Alexander Hamilton. Right: Portrait of Thomas Jefferson.

CONTENTS

Introduction   5

Chapter 1   A Nation Searches for Answers   8

Chapter 2   The People Behind the Pen Names   17

Chapter 3   Inside the Federalist Papers   26

Chapter 4   The Federalist Papers Continue   35

Chapter 5   A Close Look at the
            Anti-Federalist Perspective   42

Primary Source Transcriptions   51
Timeline   56
Glossary   57
For More Information   58
For Further Reading   59
Bibliography   60
Primary Source Image List   61
Index   62

Alexander Hamilton was the leader of the Federalists. After the United States Constitution was approved by the Constitutional Convention in 1787, he worked hard to make sure that the states approved it. Charles Willson Peale created this portrait of Hamilton in the early 1790s.

Although Thomas Jefferson did not write any of the Anti-Federalist essays, he was the leader of the group who opposed the ratification of the Constitution.

INTRODUCTION

Many of the most famous moments in history are just that—moments. A speech or a debate, however powerful and moving, is usually over in matter of a few hours or less. An exception to this rule can clearly be seen in the late 1700s. It was already a time of tremendous change in this country. The American Revolution was over, and a new beginning was at hand. While it was an exhilarating time, it was also a difficult one. There are few examples that demonstrate this period as well as the debate that raged between the two groups of political activists known as the Federalists and the Anti-Federalists.

Instead of lasting just a few hours or even days, the arguments exchanged between these two groups went on for six months. This debate took the form of writing, appearing regularly within various cities' newspapers, rather than of speech. Readers were enrapt, following each parry and thrust as if they were watching a fencing match. However, they were never quite sure whose words they were reading because not one of the messages was actually signed. The names printed at the bottom of these enthusiastic and emotional essays were not the real names of the writers. The authors used pen names to protect their identities. As politicians of this time period were known to do, they often called on Greek and Roman history to select their pseudonyms. The names they used included Brutus, Publius, Cinncinatus, Agrippa, and Cato.

The people on the two sides of this lengthy debate were passionate about their opinions. The topic under debate—the political structure of the new nation—was certainly an important one. It called for a great deal of thought, questioning, scrutiny, and deliberation.

After the American Revolution ended, the founders' first attempt at organizing the country under the Articles of Confederation was widely seen as inadequate. Consequently, the people were faced with one of the most daunting challenges possible. They were looking for a way to balance a general aversion to a powerful central government with the need for an effective system of governance that would unite all the states and the people. The issues this brought up were almost limitless. What would the laws be and how would they be enforced? Who would rule this new land? How would the people protect the very rights and freedom for which so many had just fought and died? How could the majority rule without stamping out the voices of the minority? What kind of government did Americans want now that they had won the battle against Great Britain and actually had a choice? Making such huge decisions was equally exciting and intimidating. The greatest minds of that time were immersed in trying to answer these profound and complicated questions.

Of course, there were different opinions about what type of government was needed. Some people were adamant that a strong central government with a great deal of control was necessary to prevent anarchy (no political authority at all). They soon became known as the Federalists. Almost as many people disagreed, believing that they had just escaped from an overly powerful central government and did not want to be party to forming and living under another one. They wanted the central government to have a few basic responsibilities, of course.

However, they wanted the majority of power to stay within the individual states. This way, there would be no risk of tyranny (a form of government in which a single person or organization holds complete power). They were called the Anti-Federalists. The differences between the two factions became a monumental issue in 1787 when the Constitution was written. Suddenly, it was time to decide precisely what rights and abilities the nation's government would and would not have. The American people were clearly divided.

Both sides had valid arguments and concerns, and they knew how to express those thoughts quite well. Each side was made up of very educated men, including prominent scholars, politicians, judges, and lawyers. They were also articulate men, capable of writing out and sharing their thoughts about the issues. The Federalists included well-known figures such as James Madison and Alexander Hamilton. The Anti-Federalists had members such as Thomas Jefferson and Patrick Henry.

For six months, as the Constitution entered the ratification process, both the Federalists and Anti-Federalists publicly debated the many elements contained in it. In the end, their words became some of history's most authoritative texts on what the United States is about and what principles it holds most dear.

The debate over the level of federal authority has stubbornly remained with the country as time passes. Heated arguments over some of the same issues raised between the Federalists and Anti-Federalists can still be spotted in the newspapers or heard on political talk shows. How much control should government have over the individual person? How much can people rely on the rights spelled out in the Constitution and how much do they have to keep fighting to retain them? Is the Constitution perfect the way it is or does it still, more than two centuries later, need some work? These are simple questions with complex answers and no one is certain when—or if—they will ever be permanently settled.

CHAPTER 1

A NATION SEARCHES FOR ANSWERS

Starting a new country was no small chore. The Americans faced with that challenge following the Revolutionary War had their hands full. The last half of the eighteenth century was an extraordinarily exciting time in the country's history. The Revolutionary War had ended, and people had broken away from England's control at last. Now that they had what they wanted and what they had fought so hard for—their freedom—they were not entirely sure how to handle it. The greatest minds of the time were concentrating on deciding the ideal ways to fashion a nation and determine how it should be governed. They knew they did not want the British system. However, without any other models to go by, they were not sure how to organize their government.

The Articles of Confederation

It did not take long before issues began to pop up that proved to people that some kind of government was needed within the thirteen states. In 1777, a document called the Articles of Confederation was drafted. Four years later, it was ratified.

This 1883 engraving by H. A. Ogden portrays the disbanding of a major part of the Continental army in New Windsor, New York, 100 years earlier. The Continental army was disbanded in November 1783, two months after the signing of the Treaty of Paris, which ended the American Revolution.

As the first official constitution of the United States, it was the main set of rules and regulations that guided the new states through their first few struggling years.

Deciding what would go into this first constitution was not an easy process. Every decision seemed to require long, detailed debates. In the end, the Articles of Confederation established a permanent national congress, made up of two to seven delegates from each of the thirteen states. There was no executive or judicial branch yet. Congress would be empowered to declare war or peace, handle foreign relations, and keep an army and navy. Ironically, it could create laws,

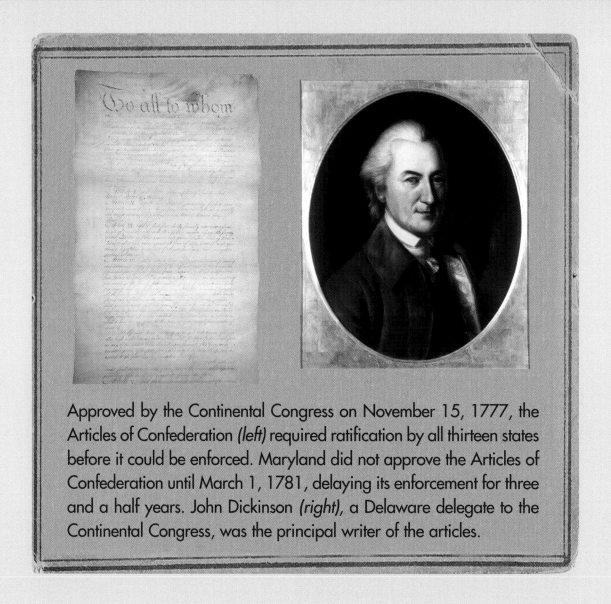

Approved by the Continental Congress on November 15, 1777, the Articles of Confederation *(left)* required ratification by all thirteen states before it could be enforced. Maryland did not approve the Articles of Confederation until March 1, 1781, delaying its enforcement for three and a half years. John Dickinson *(right)*, a Delaware delegate to the Continental Congress, was the principal writer of the articles.

yet it could not enforce them. The states could simply choose whether they wanted to go along with Congress's directives. The Articles of Confederation was also the first national document to take an official stand against slavery, offering all men the same basic rights.

In 1787, Congress enacted an important piece of legislation called the Northwest Ordinance. This law was established to describe exactly how new states would be formed from the various lands won in the Revolutionary War. The northwest region, the area between the Ohio and Mississippi Rivers and by the Great Lakes, was split up into territories, and governors, judges, and secretaries were appointed for each one. (The role of the secretaries was to maintain the public records.) The ordinance established that once a territory reached a population of 5,000 adult men, the territory could elect a representative to Congress. When the population reached 60,000 adult men, it could officially apply for statehood. (The number of women, nonwhites, and children at that time was considered irrelevant.)

In the beginning, the Articles of Confederation was adequate for the new states. It described the relationship between the states as a "firm league of friendship." It had not, however, created a union as had been hoped. Instead, the states were considered to be connected by what George Washington referred to as "a rope of sand," in a February 28, 1785, letter to Henry Knox. In other words, the union was not very strong. It quickly became obvious that the system of governance that was laid out in the Articles of Confederation was inadequate to meet the growing needs of the new country. The individual states began to demand changes, and slowly the document began to be watered down with various revisions and amendments. Something more structured and extensive was needed.

The Northwest Ordinance set up a three-step procedure for converting the Northwest Territory into American states. It also created a bill of rights for settlers, encouraged education, and outlawed slavery.

SHAYS'S REBELLION

In the late summer of 1786, a farmer and former Revolutionary Army captain named Daniel Shays led a rebellion in Massachusetts. Tired of the unfair ways in which he felt the current laws and government were treating workers and farmers like himself, he led others to protest by storming the courthouses in several cities. Shays wanted to see changes in the nation's judicial system. He was prepared to use violence to push for reform. For several months, Shays and his followers attacked court buildings where those living in poverty had been treated badly or even imprisoned. Finally, in early 1787, the militia captured him and 2,000 of his men. They were sentenced to death for treason, but were later pardoned.

Massachusetts appealed to the federal government for help. However, the federal government was powerless to act under the Articles of Confederation. It was yet another example of the need to revise the articles.

Replacing the Articles

In 1786, a group of businessmen met in Annapolis, Maryland, to talk about some problems they had been having with commerce that involved people in different states. As they discussed the issues, they began to realize that business was only the beginning of the problems. It was obvious that the new nation was outgrowing the Articles of Confederation. It seemed like each person had a question or issue that was not covered by the articles, and so they were not sure what to do

This illustration from the 1787 *Bickerstaff's Boston Almanack* provides the only known image of Daniel Shays (portrayed at left). Shays was born in Hopkinton, Massachusetts, in 1747. During the American Revolution, he achieved the rank of captain in the Continental army.

about it. Finally, they decided to hold a convention to explore either a complete revision of the articles or the creation of a similar document that had a wider scope.

In May 1787, a group of delegates gathered in Philadelphia once again to take a slow, careful, and thoughtful look at the Articles of Confederation and to decide what was needed. They wanted to find a way to unite the thirteen states. George Washington was elected president of what was called the Constitutional Convention. His diplomatic skills were well known and would be well tested during this event. Many different plans and ideas were suggested, some with great heat and passion.

IN THE EAGLE'S BEAK

On the Great Seal of the United States of America, there is an eagle with a ribbon in its beak. Written on the ribbon is the Latin phrase, *e pluribus unum*, which is attributed to the Roman poet Virgil. It means "out of many, one" and was the motto for the confederation of delegates who organized the Articles of Confederation.

However, the delegates generally realized that the occasion called for calm and tact to keep it under control as everything was suggested, discussed, and then either accepted or rejected.

The Virginia Plan, for instance, proposed that the country have a bicameral (two-house) legislature. It also suggested that a state's representation in the federal government should be based on the population or wealth of the state. This was upsetting to delegates from the smaller states, who feared that this arrangement would not give them the level of representation they wanted. The New Jersey Plan made another suggestion: states would have equal representation, but there would be a Supreme Court. Connecticut suggested the final compromise between the plans. The country would have a bicameral legislature. The upper house would be the Senate. In it, each state would have equal representation. The lower house would be the House of Representatives. There, representation would be based on the population of the state. The new government would also have a Supreme Court and a complex system of checks and balances built into it. This would ensure that no one branch of

Entitled *Convention at Philadelphia*, this engraving portrays George Washington addressing a group of delegates at the Constitutional Convention in 1787. Of the fifty-five delegates who attended the convention, only thirty-nine signed the resulting Constitution. Washington, a delegate from Virginia, was one of the signers.

government would have too much power. For every power granted to one branch of government, the others would have the ability to stop or check it.

A Complex Task

Putting together the actual Constitution of the United States was an incredibly complicated procedure. Arguments emerged constantly, and educated and dedicated men debated issue after issue. It slowly came together, incorporating many different ideas, until some people began to refer to it as a "bundle of compromises." Finally, the document was completed, and it was time for the next big step: ratification. Nine of the thirteen states had to approve the new Constitution before it could become official. It was a procedure that took three years to accomplish. While some states—like Delaware, New Jersey, and Georgia—agreed almost immediately, other states were slower to respond. Certain issues were still being debated. As more people began to speak out against various provisions of the new document, strong advocates of the Constitution began to worry. The country seemed equally divided between those who agreed and those who disagreed with the Constitution.

Four weeks after the Constitution was presented for ratification, an essay explaining why all the states should approve it appeared in the *Independent Journal*. It focused on the document's integrity. Shortly after, a rebuttal appeared—and a new form of national debate was born. In print, essay by essay, week by week, the two political groups that would come to be known as the Federalists and the Anti-Federalists shared their hopes, worries, thoughts, and comments about the future of the nation with all of its citizens.

CHAPTER 2

THE PEOPLE BEHIND THE PEN NAMES

The ongoing debate between the Federalists and Anti-Federalists was unique within history. Not only was it in writing, but it lasted for six months. It involved almost a dozen people, most of whom hid their true identities. Who were the mysterious writers behind the hundreds of essays that appeared in newspapers, including New York's *Independent Journal* and *Poughkeepsie Country Journal*, Philadelphia's *Freeman's Journal*, and Boston's *American Herald*? Years after the essays were written and the Constitution had been ratified, the people responsible for these commentaries continued to deny their involvement. It has taken almost an entire century for historians to finally figure out exactly who the authors were and how many essays each wrote.

The Federalists

Without a doubt, between the two political groups, the Federalists were more organized and effective in presenting their side of the debate. Their eighty-five essays were quite orderly, and although there were three primary writers, each one attempted to imitate the others' styles so as to appear as one writer. Although it has not been proven, historians suspect the men read each other's work and discussed what needed to be written next.

The first person to develop the idea of a series of newspaper articles supporting the ratification of the Constitution was Alexander Hamilton. A former special aide and personal friend to George Washington, he already had a great deal of experience as a writer of newspaper essays and pamphlets. Hamilton represented New York at the convention in Annapolis and was one of the people responsible for arranging the ensuing Constitutional Convention in 1786.

Hamilton wanted to see a strong central government in place in the United States. He felt that ratification of the new Constitution was the primary way to achieve that. He was a strong believer in organization and order and feared that if the Constitution was not adopted, the new nation would see complete lawlessness. Businessmen supported Hamilton because he encouraged the ideas of a large national bank and mint that supported commerce and industrial development.

Hamilton wanted to help ensure that the necessary nine states ratified the Constitution, so he came up with the idea of writing essays for the newspapers. He was not sure that he could do it alone, however, so he turned to some of his colleagues and asked for their help. The first person he asked for help was John Jay. In the end, Hamilton wrote fifty-one of the eighty-five Federalist essays.

Jay had been one of the main people involved in negotiating peace with Great Britain at the end of the Revolutionary War. Under the Articles of Confederation, he was the secretary for foreign affairs. When Hamilton asked him to write some essays about foreign policy for the newspapers, he agreed. Because of poor health, he wrote only

John Jay was born in New York City on December 12, 1745. At first, he did not support independence from Britain. However, he threw his support behind the colonies once the revolution was underway. He was president of the Continental Congress between 1778 and 1779 and held other high-ranking positions throughout the revolutionary period. After the Constitution was ratified, he became the first chief justice of the United States.

A ROMAN ROLE MODEL

All three Federalists signed their essays with the name Publius. This was in honor of an ancient Roman statesman named Publius Valerius Publicola. He was their inspiration because he had once helped establish the Roman republic and warned Roman citizens of any possible threats to their freedom.

five essays. However, they were important ones. They dealt primarily with the international advantages of adopting the Constitution.

Next, Hamilton asked Gouverneur Morris to join the Federalist team, but he declined. He had a strong background in law, and the 173 speeches he had made during the Constitutional Convention had made a strong impression on Hamilton. Morris was one of the main people to draft the Constitution. Hamilton had hoped he would add his prolific thoughts to the series of essays. However, Morris was deeply involved in his business and could not spare the time.

A man named William Duer was asked to join the Federalists. He was the assistant secretary to Hamilton at the time. He submitted three essays for the Federalists. Hamilton rejected each one and was forced to find one more writer. This time he selected James Madison, a future president of the United States.

Madison was sometimes called the father of the Constitution because of the dedication and faith he put into it. Although George Washington was elected president of the Constitutional Convention, it

James Madison *(left)* was a leading voice at the Constitutional Convention. Some of his favorite ideas became central features of the eventual Constitution. These include separation of powers, a strong legislature, and an independent judiciary. He was also a primary force behind the creation of the Library of Congress. A page from his notes from a congressional debate on the subject is pictured at right.

was actually Madison who acted as primary leader. He accepted the Federalists' offer and ended up writing twenty-six essays. He also cowrote three essays with Hamilton. This was not an easy process since the two men did not always see eye to eye on some issues, even though they were both Federalists.

The Anti-Federalists

The Anti-Federalists were not as structured as their opponents. However, they were just as passionate about their beliefs. Instead of multiple writers using one pen name, each person took his own pseudonym. Although their leader was often considered to be Thomas Jefferson, he did not write any of the Anti-Federalist essays.

Centinel

The most prolific of the Anti-Federalist writers was Centinel. He wrote a total of twenty-four essays between October 1787 and November 1788. Most of these were published in Philadelphia newspapers. His main focus was on the system of checks and balances that had been built into the Constitution. Historians believe that Centinel was most likely a man named Samuel Bryan, the owner of several Philadelphia newspapers.

Brutus

Another frequent writer was Brutus. His sixteen articles appeared in New York's *Independent Journal.* They were widely reprinted in other newspapers. Each one was addressed to "the Citizens of the State of New York." Brutus was probably a man named Robert Yates, a New York judge. He chose the name to honor the Roman who killed Julius Caesar. Experts believe that he also wrote under the name of Sydney.

The Federal Farmer

The Federal Farmer wrote thirteen essays for the Anti-Federalists. Most of them were printed in New York's *Poughkeepsie Country Journal.* He is thought to be either Richard Henry Lee, a delegate from Virginia, or Melancton Smith, a delegate from New York.

The Rest of the Club

Other writers were Cato, most likely New York governor George Clinton, and Cincinnatus, New Yorker Arthur Lee. Additional pen

Richard Henry Lee was born in Westmoreland County, Virginia, on January 20, 1732. He was one of the signers of the Declaration of Independence. He was not a delegate of the Constitutional Convention. Lee worried that the Constitution gave the central government too much power. He argued strongly against Virginia ratifying the Constitution before certain amendments were made. In 1789, he became Virginia's first senator under the Constitution.

Mercy Otis Warren was the only female contributor to the debate between the Federalists and Anti-Federalists. Born in Barnstable, Massachusetts, in 1728, she was one of the most educated women of her time. She was the author of several plays, some of which were propaganda pieces against the colonial government. In 1805, she published the three-volume *History of the American Revolution.*

names used by other writers included Philanthropos, Montezuma, Candidus, Leonidas, Aristocrotis, and Republicus. Letters by a Columbian Patriot actually came from the pen of a woman, Mercy Warren, sister of another Anti-Federalist named James who signed his letters either Republican Federalist or Helvidius Priscus. A few authors even signed their real names, including Virginia governor Patrick Henry, Virginia colonel William Grayson, and William Penn, the founder of Pennsylvania.

Like the Federalists, the Anti-Federalists wrote more than eighty essays. When today's readers look at any of these essays, regardless of which side of the issue they come from, it is obvious that there is a great deal of repetition within them. New essays were being published as often as four times a week. Frequently, they were reprinted in a half-dozen different newspapers. It's important to remember that when both sides penned these essays, they never imagined they would

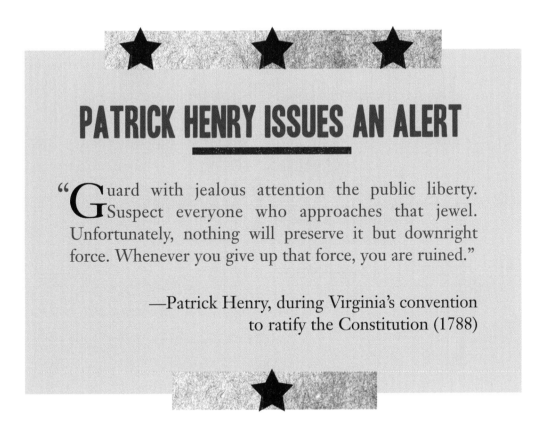

PATRICK HENRY ISSUES AN ALERT

"Guard with jealous attention the public liberty. Suspect everyone who approaches that jewel. Unfortunately, nothing will preserve it but downright force. Whenever you give up that force, you are ruined."

—Patrick Henry, during Virginia's convention
to ratify the Constitution (1788)

be gathered together into a book and read one after another. Instead, the essays were part of an ongoing series with days and sometimes weeks between them. In some ways, they were like a sophisticated advertising campaign in which each side kept running an advertisement of sorts, with obvious repetition to help the readers—or customers— remember the important points.

CHAPTER 3

INSIDE THE FEDERALIST PAPERS

As the Constitution went before each state for ratification, Madison, Hamilton, and Jay geared up for one of the most intense episodes of propaganda that history has ever seen. Together, the men wrote eighty-five essays designed to do nothing other than show the people the wisdom of ratifying the Constitution. They saw the Constitution as the way to achieve that perfect union so many desired. The first thirty-six papers were written to highlight the inadequacies of the current Articles of Confederation. Essays 37 through 85 highlighted the different elements built into the Constitution and why they would benefit the nation. They told the people that this new government was the only way to achieve the peace and security for which they had all just fought. According to the Federalists, the Constitution meant growth in national power, eventual prosperity, and complete independence.

Today, the Federalist Papers are considered the definitive source for scholars on the true intentions of the Constitution. Because the famous and powerful document did not provide people with any explanations and justifications for what was in it, these three men filled in the gaps. Also, through their letters to the newspapers, they told people why certain provisions had or had not been included or what changes had been made. It was a marvelous and unique opportunity to sell the people on big government, one letter at a time.

The language in which the Federalist Papers were written leaves little doubt in the reader's mind that the authors were educated men. However, it also made the essays somewhat challenging for some people to understand. The English language was much more formal 200 years ago than it is today, especially when it came to politics. Looking at the first two sentences of the "General Introduction," the first of the Federalist essays, might send many of today's readers scrambling for a dictionary. Alexander Hamilton wrote:

> After an unequivocal experience of the inefficacy of the subsisting federal government, you are called upon to deliberate on a new Constitution for the United States of America. The subject speaks its own importance: comprehending the consequences nothing less than the existence of the UNION, the safety and welfare of the parts of which it is composed, the fate of an empire in many respects the most interesting in the world.

Despite the difficult vocabulary, the "General Introduction" remains passionate and strong more than two centuries after it was written. In it, Hamilton outlined what he had planned to do in the essays to follow. Originally, he and the other writers had estimated that there would be between twenty and twenty-five pieces total. It was a surprise to them when they ended up with more than three times that amount.

THE GREATEST SOURCE

" I f it be asked, What is the most sacred duty and the greatest source of our security in a Republic? The answer would be, An inviolable respect for the constitution and Laws."

—Alexander Hamilton in an essay published in the *American Daily Advertiser*, August 28, 1794

The Essays Begin

The first set of Federalist essays outlined the many ways in which the Articles of Confederation was no longer adequate for their new nation. They pointed out its weaknesses again and again, each from a slightly different angle. It was a wise way to begin their side of the debate, because most people agreed with them—the articles were no longer sufficient and needed revision. In John Jay's essays, he pointed out the similarities of the people, once again, emphasizing what everyone had in common. He listed everything from belief in the same God and use of the same language to use of the same land and the same trading system. In his second essay, he encouraged the people to use "sober consideration" instead of "blind acceptance" when it came to choosing a form of government.

From the sixth essay on, the tone changed to a more serious and demanding one. In essays 6 and 8, Hamilton wrote that he wanted a united country because he feared "frequent and violent contests" between the states otherwise. It was clear that Hamilton truly worried

The New-York Packet.

Tros Tyriusque nobis nullo Discrimine agetur. Virg.

TUESDAY, NOVEMBER 20, 1787.

[Nº 751.]

This November 20, 1787, edition of *The New-York Packet* carried Federalist Papers essays 7 and 8, both written by Alexander Hamilton *(inset)*. In them, Hamilton argued that a strong federal government was needed to serve as an umpire in disputes between the states. He feared that without a strong federal government, states could go to war against each other over issues such as border disputes and commerce.

that, without some form of strong and powerful central government, the country would fall apart. Because he felt that the smaller states would be overtaken by the larger ones, he thought that the nation must have a standing army to prevent this situation from happening. Many of the Federalists' essays often covered the topic of states' safety over and over because it was a concern that many people shared. In essay 9, Hamilton compared the nation and the individual states with the sun and the planets that orbit around it. He used the analogy to show that just as the planets depend on the big and powerful sun for survival, so should the states revolve around a government for their survival. "A firm Union will be of the utmost moment to the peace and liberty of the states as a barrier against domestic faction and insurrection," he wrote.

The tenth essay was written by James Madison. It is considered one of the most effective of the entire series. He reminded people that establishing a government would help control the violence and damage that can be caused by factions, or people who gather to protect their own personal economic or political interests. Madison wrote:

A zeal for different opinions concerning religion, concerning government and many other points, as well of speculation as of practice; an attachment to different leaders ambitiously contending for preeminence and power; or two persons of other descriptions whose fortunes have been interesting to the human passions, have, in turn, divided mankind into parties, inflamed them with mutual animosity and rendered them much more disposed to vex and oppress each other than to cooperate for their common good.

Essays 15 and 16 changed the tone of the papers once more. National safety was put aside, and Hamilton focused again on the

In New York, the Federalists found one of the strongest opponents to the Constitution in Governor George Clinton. Clinton wrote seven letters in which he argued against the adoption of the Constitution. Three of these are counted among the Anti-Federalist essays. Ironically, Clinton presided over New York's convention that ratified the federal Constitution. He was twice elected vice president of the United States.

"insufficiency of present confederation to the preservation of the union." He painted a rather dire picture of the country, bringing up sensitive issues such as its large debts incurred during the war, its low property values, its poor standing with other countries, and its lack of military and underdeveloped commercial sector. He reminded readers that the Federalists felt that government existed because men do not reliably conform to the "dictates of reason and justice." His party always felt that groups would act more responsibly and intelligently than individuals would. He referred to the Articles of Confederation as "the parent of anarchy" and returned to the issue of the need to keep

THE RATIFICATION OF THE CONSTITUTION

This is the order in which the states agreed to the Constitution and how the votes were divided.

State	Date	Vote Count
Delaware	December 7, 1787	30–0
Pennsylvania	December 12, 1787	46–23
New Jersey	December 18, 1787	38–0
Georgia	January 2, 1788	26–0
Connecticut	January 9, 1788	128–40
Massachusetts	February 6, 1788	187–168
Maryland	April 28, 1788	63–11
South Carolina	May 23, 1788	149–73
New Hampshire	June 21, 1788	57–47
Virginia	June 25, 1788	89–79
New York	July 26, 1788	30–27
North Carolina	November 21, 1789	194–77
Rhode Island	May 29, 1790	34–32

This engraving examines the rift in Connecticut politics on the eve of the ratification of the federal Constitution. It portrays the Federalists as commercial traders and the Anti-Federalists as farmers. Connecticut is represented by a wagon being pulled in opposite directions by the two sides. The wagon is sinking under a load of debt and paper money into mud. Its driver warns, "Gentlemen this Machine is deep in the mire and you are divided as to its [relief]."

harmony between the states. The government must "carry its agency to the persons of the citizens," he wrote.

Hamilton added in essay 22 that a strong central government would be the answer to the commercial problems of most companies. Without a strong central government, it was understandable that foreign governments were hesitant to do business with the United States. They feared that there would be hostility between the states, and according to Hamilton, the Articles of Confederation was considered "radically vicious and unsound." Before concluding, he turned to one other issue that the articles had not addressed—judiciary power. As he so eloquently phrased it, "Laws are a dead letter without courts to expound and define their true meaning and operation." He discussed what he called the Supreme Tribunal, or what is now known as the Supreme Court. Knowing that different courts and different judges often came up with different styles of ruling, he stated:

> To avoid the confusion which would unavoidably result from the contradictory decisions of a number of independent judicatories [judiciaries], all nations have found it necessary to establish one court paramount to the rest, possessing a general superintendence and authorized to settle and declare in the last resort a uniform rule of civil justice.

The first twenty-two Federalist essays achieved exactly what the authors had intended. They showed readers the flaws and dangers of the current government. They also set the scene for the next barrage of letters, which would show the perfect solution: ratification of the Constitution.

CHAPTER 4

THE FEDERALIST PAPERS CONTINUE

Having accomplished their goal of pointing out the defects and imperfections of the Articles of Confederation, the Federalists turned their attention to the second part of their propaganda. They wanted to persuade Americans that the nation needed an energetic government that represented true republican principles. In addition, the authors wanted readers to learn about two integral features of the Constitution: the separation of powers and the system of checks and balances.

Essays 23 through 36 were written by Alexander Hamilton. All of them focused on the importance of having an energetic government, backed by a firm and clear Constitution. In essay 37, Madison, writing his first essay, made his primary point that there was a thin line between trying to guarantee people liberty while still maintaining authority over them. He wrote, "Energy in government is essential to that security against external and internal danger and to that prompt and salutary execution of the law, which enter into the very definition of good government. Stability in government is essential to national character.

At left is George Washington's copy of the Virginia Plan. James Madison had proposed many of its ideas to Washington before the Constitutional Convention was held. The engraving at right portrays Washington's inauguration as the first president of the United States in 1789.

On comparing, however, these valuable ingredients with the vital principles of liberty, we must perceive at once the difficulty of mingling them in their due proportions."

What precisely is a republican government based on, and how did the new Constitution meet those requirements? Those were the questions Madison set out to answer, beginning with essay 39. This new discussion brought in special terminology for readers. In essay 47, Madison talked about a specific element found in republican governments called "separation of powers." The Constitution called for three separate branches of government (legislative, executive, and judicial), and some people were concerned that the branches were not separate enough from each other. They also worried that the power was not evenly distributed among them. Madison understood this and even stated that too much power in one branch "is the very definition of tyranny." In essay 47, Madison told the people how each branch would work and what abilities it might have. This introduced the concept of "checks and balances" or the capability of one branch to have power over the actions of the other branches. This process stops any one branch from having too much power.

Madison's essay 51 is considered to be one of the most important of all. He set out to clearly explain to people how the government would make liberty possible for everyone. He addressed the issue of class struggle and politics when he wrote, "It is of great importance in a republic not only to guard against the oppression of its rulers, but to guard one part of the society against the injustice of the other. Different interests necessarily exist in different classes of citizens . . . If a majority be united by a common interest the rights of the minority will be secure."

In essays 62 and 63, Madison discussed some of the more detailed information found in the new Constitution, particularly within the

This is the March 28, 1788, edition of *The New-York Packet*. It carried essay 74, Hamilton's "The Command of the Military and Naval Forces, and pardoning Power of the Executive."

Senate. He wrote about the qualification of senators, the method used to elect them, the concept of equal representation, the number of senators, and the length of their terms. In essay 70, Hamilton began discussing what character traits it takes to be a president and lead the country. The Federalists wanted to make sure people knew that the president was not going to lead America like the king had ruled England. He would not be immune from criticism, accountability, or even disciplinary action. Unlike royalty, the president would not be a sacred figure. Even today, this specific essay is read if there is any question about what powers the president does and does not have.

In essay 78, Hamilton continued to educate the public about the details of the proposed Constitution. The judicial branch, considered to be the weakest branch, is the focus of this essay. Hamilton wrote, "A constitution is, in fact, and must be regarded by the judged, as a fundamental law." Hamilton believed that federal judges should hold their offices for life. After all, many laws are complex, and it could take years to fully understand their meaning. Essay 79 continued the same topic and discussed how judges should be compensated for their work. The Constitution states that U.S. judges "shall at stated times receive for

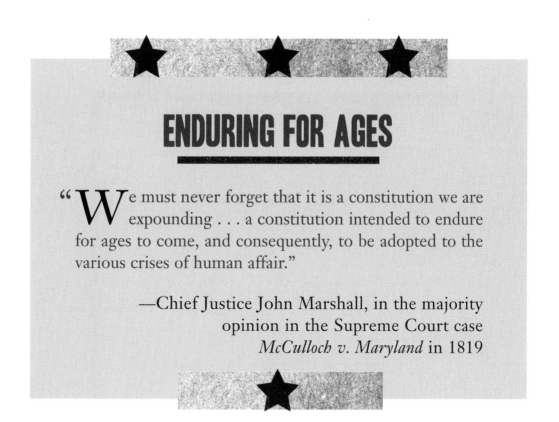

ENDURING FOR AGES

"We must never forget that it is a constitution we are expounding . . . a constitution intended to endure for ages to come, and consequently, to be adopted to the various crises of human affair."

—Chief Justice John Marshall, in the majority opinion in the Supreme Court case *McCulloch v. Maryland* in 1819

their services a compensation which shall not be diminished during their continuance in office."

A Few Last Objections

Hamilton wrote the last two essays of the Federalist Papers. In essay 84, he admitted that there were still some objections to the Constitution that he had not fully addressed. One of the main issues was the lack of a bill of rights. This was a much debated topic and one of the primary reasons several states were hesitant to agree to ratification. Hamilton attempted to show in this essay that despite the lack of an actual bill of rights, people did not need to worry that their interests were not going to be protected. He listed the six safeguards built into the Constitution, including separation of powers and checks and balances. There was an unspoken philosophy that creating a bill of rights could backfire on the government. Listing the specific rights that were going to be protected could encourage people to propose additional rights.

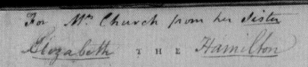

For Mrs Church from her sister Elizabeth THE *Hamilton*

FEDERALIST:

A COLLECTION

OF

ESSAYS,

WRITTEN IN FAVOUR OF THE

NEW CONSTITUTION,

AS AGREED UPON BY THE FEDERAL CONVENTION,
SEPTEMBER 17, 1787.

IN TWO VOLUMES.

VOL. I.

NEW-YORK:

PRINTED AND SOLD BY J. AND A. M'LEAN,
No. 41, HANOVER-SQUARE.
M,DCC,LXXXVIII.

Mr Jefferson's copy

This is the first edition of *The Federalist: A Collection of Essays, Written in Favour of the New Constitution.* It was published in New York in 1788 by J. and A. McLean. This copy was first owned by Alexander Hamilton's wife, Elizabeth. It later came under the ownership of Thomas Jefferson, who noted the author of each essay on a flyleaf in the book.

In the last essay, Hamilton asked readers if he did what he said he would do in the first essay—prove that the Constitution was a benefit to the nation. He reminded each man that reading and understanding this information was essential, as was making the right decision afterward. He wrote:

Let us now pause and ask ourselves whether, in the course of these papers, the proposed Constitution has not been satisfactorily vindicated from the aspersions thrown upon it; and whether it has not been shown to be worthy of the public approbation and necessary to the public safety and prosperity. Every man is bound to answer these questions to himself, according to the best of his conscience and understanding, and to act agreeably to the genuine and sober dictates of his judgment. This is a duty from which nothing can give him a dispensation. 'Tis the one he is called upon, nay, constrained by all the obligations that form the bands of society, to discharge sincerely and honestly.

Finally, the Federalists were done. For six months their essays had appeared in various newspapers. Madison, Hamilton, and Jay had done what they had intended to do with those words. The people of the new nation had a better idea of what the Constitution might include and why it was written the way it was. Although that helped many people to make up their minds, there were still a great many who still had some questions and objections. They were the people who had also kept up with the opposing opinions being published and found themselves agreeing with these viewpoints. These were the Anti-Federalists. They too had made reasonable and passionate arguments in this lengthy debate.

CHAPTER 5

A CLOSE LOOK AT THE ANTI-FEDERALIST PERSPECTIVE

While the Federalists were busy writing their essays and gathering as much momentum as possible behind the ratification of the Constitution, there were many scholars and other educated men who were asking questions and raising multiple objections. They did not feel that a republican form of government would work on a national scale. They also worried that people's rights were going to be insufficiently protected. Although they came to be called the Anti-Federalists, they thought of themselves more as the patriots who were carrying out the same spirit that had begun with the Revolution.

Assembling the Cast

Led in part by Thomas Jefferson, the Anti-Federalists were made up of a variety of men. They all shared the concern that this new Constitution would give far too much power to the central government, instead of letting the individual states make most of the decisions. The Anti-Federalists rejected the idea of people looking to a huge, strong primary government

Thomas Jefferson *(left)* was an ardent Anti-Federalist, even though he did not write any of the essays against ratifying the U.S. Constitution. His vision of the United States often clashed with that of Alexander Hamilton, the leader of the Federalists. Their disagreements lasted long after the Constitution was ratified. In this July 7, 1793, letter, he urges James Madison to attack Hamilton's ideas.

for what they needed. They believed in putting responsibility on the individual, not some glorious empire. Anti-Federalists trusted people to be decent and honest. They worried that the Federalists' image of government would eventually lead to tyranny and a never-ending desire for additional power. A central government would not have any real connection to the people, they argued. They worried that, under this new government, the president would become like the king they had just rejected. Similarly, they were concerned that the rich would be given more benefits than the poor, just as the big states would profit more than little ones. Anti-Federalists were also concerned that the Constitution

43

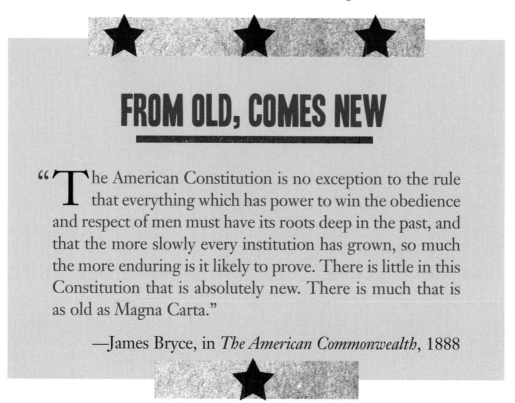

FROM OLD, COMES NEW

"The American Constitution is no exception to the rule that everything which has power to win the obedience and respect of men must have its roots deep in the past, and that the more slowly every institution has grown, so much the more enduring is it likely to prove. There is little in this Constitution that is absolutely new. There is much that is as old as Magna Carta."

—James Bryce, in *The American Commonwealth*, 1888

contained no bill of rights. Many people had lost their lives and fought hard against England in the Revolutionary War to earn those rights, so they wanted to make sure they kept them. Many of the essays the Anti-Federalists wrote focused on the lack of a bill of rights, and some of the states refused to agree to the ratification process without one. In 1791, one was created and added to the Constitution.

The differences between the two parties were actually simple. The Federalists believed that humans needed to be controlled. The Anti-Federalists felt they needed to be set free.

Unlike the Federalist Papers, which were written in an orderly fashion by three men, the Anti-Federalist essays were written by almost a dozen people and with far less organization. This hurt their movement and it is clear in looking back on the documents that they were on the losing side. They did not have the unified plans and actions their opponents did. The language used was slightly simpler, written more for working-class readers. An essay written under the pseudonym John

This is the January 10, 1788, edition of the *New-York Journal and Weekly Register*. It carried the eighth Anti-Federalist essay written by Brutus. In it, he objected to the federal government's wide power to borrow money and to raise a federal army. It was a rebuttal to Federalist essay 23 by Alexander Hamilton.

DeWitt responded to the Federalists' attitude that adopting the Constitution would take care of all of the nation's problems. DeWitt wrote:

We are told by some people, that upon the adopting [of] this New Government, we are to become the every thing in a Moment:—Our foreign and domestic debts will be as a Feather; our ports will be crowded with the ships of all the world, soliciting our commerce and our produce: Our manufacturers will increase and multiply; and, in short, if we STAND STILL, our country, notwithstanding, will be like the blessed Canaan, a land flowing with milk and honey. Let us not deceive ourselves; the only excellency of any government is in exact proportion to the administration of it:—Idleness and luxury will be as much a bane was ever: our passions will be equally at war with us then as now; and if we have men among us trying with all their ability to undermine our present Constitution, these very persons will direct their force to sap the vitals of the new one.

Bring in the Amendments

One of the primary ways that the Anti-Federalists battled the Constitution was by proposing a variety of amendments that they felt were necessary. Some were simple, while others were considered to be radical, especially those proposed by Rhode Island, the last state to agree to the Constitution. Rhode Island representatives strongly objected to the idea of keeping a standing army and wanted to ensure that Congress could not declare war without the approval of two-thirds of the senators and representatives.

The Federal Farmer

One of the most outspoken Anti-Federalists was the so-called Federal Farmer. His essays have been considered some of the most eloquent and persuasive. In letters published in the *Poughkeepsie Country Journal*, he wrote about the possibility of slowing down and taking time to think things over carefully before making the decision to ratify the Constitution. Since the Federalists had repeatedly focused on safety issues in their essays, he decided to address the question from that perspective. He argued,

If we remain cool and temperate, we are in no immediate danger of any commotions; we are in a state of perfect peace,

Patrick Henry was one of the most vocal opponents of the United States Constitution. Henry believed that the Constitution gave the federal government too much power. Henry insisted that a bill of rights be added to the Constitution before Virginia considered approving it. This engraving by H. B. Hall portrays Henry addressing the Virginia assembly in 1765.

and in no danger of invasions; the state governments are in the full exercise of their powers; and our governments will answer all present exigencies, except the regulation of trade, securing credit, in some cases, and providing for the interest, in some instances, of the public debts; and whether we adopt a change, three or nine months hence, can make but little odds with the private circumstances of individuals; their happiness and prosperity, after all, depend principally upon their own exertions.

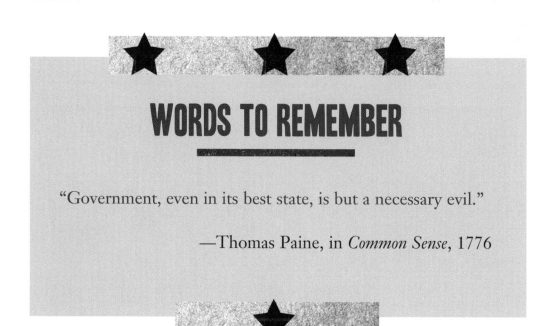

Brutus

Brutus was the main Anti-Federalist writer to work his way through the Constitution paragraph by paragraph, pointing out its problems and flaws in his essays. He urged readers to think about every element in the document and to consider whether they were truly necessary. He wrote:

> The first question that presents itself on the subject is, whether a confederated government be the best for the United States or not? Or in other words, whether the thirteen United States should be reduced to one great republic, governed by one legislature and under the direction of one executive and judicial; or whether they should continue thirteen confederated republics, under the direction and control of a supreme federal head for certain defined national purposes only?

Brutus also strongly disagreed with the idea of maintaining a permanent standing army. In one of his essays, he wrote:

> The liberties of a people are in danger from a large standing army, not only because the rulers may employ them for the

purposes of supporting themselves in any usurpations of power, which they may see proper to exercise, but there is a great hazard, that an army will subvert the forms of the government, under whose authority they are raised, and establish one according to the pleasure of their leader.

Although some might look back at this time period and think that the Anti-Federalists were the "losers" in this lengthy debate, that is not really true. While the Constitution was eventually ratified, no group actually lost this historical argument. Instead, both sides made valid points that made the opposition think and even initiate some changes. Both parties made the people think about their beliefs, their wants, and their needs. Faced with the enormous challenge of trying to create a new country, everyone did their best to make the right decisions.

A Never-ending Debate

The debate over what should fall under states' rights and national government control did not end with the ratification of the Constitution. The issue pops up repeatedly in modern times, frequently between today's Republicans and Democrats. What is legally allowed in one state is often not allowed in another. Whenever that happens, there is often discussion of letting the government take over the entire issue and make all the decisions. Recent issues that have been debated include gay marriages and homeschooling. Just like 200 years ago, there are passionate, emotional, and intelligent people on either side of the issues, and while they may not officially debate through their local newspapers like the Federalists and Anti-Federalists did, their voices are heard one way or another.

More than two centuries after the Constitution was written, people still debate its contents. Occasionally, debates over constitutional issues lead to an amendment. Twenty-six amendments have been added since the Constitution was created. The last amendment was made in 1971. People of every political persuasion will most likely continue to strive to create that perfect union, difficult as it may be. Thanks to an impressive and dedicated group of Americans who took the time to write out their thoughts many years ago, people today have clearer ideas of what went into creating the nation's set of rules and regulations.

Perhaps George Washington summed it up best when he said, "The Federalist Papers have thrown a new light upon the science of government; they have given the rights of man a full and fair discussion and explained them in so clear and forcible a manner as cannot fail to make a lasting impression."

Federalist Essay No. 47: The Particular Structure of the New Government and the Distribution of Power Among Its Different Parts

From *The New-York Packet*, Friday, February 1, 1788.

To the People of the State of New York:

HAVING reviewed the general form of the proposed government and the general mass of power allotted to it, I proceed to examine the particular structure of this government, and the distribution of this mass of power among its constituent parts. One of the principal objections inculcated by the more respectable adversaries to the Constitution, is its supposed violation of the political maxim, that the legislative, executive, and judiciary departments ought to be separate and distinct. In the structure of the federal government, no regard, it is said, seems to have been paid to this essential precaution in favor of liberty. The several departments of power are distributed and blended in such a manner as at once to destroy all symmetry and beauty of form, and to expose some of the essential parts of the edifice to the danger of being crushed by the disproportionate weight of other parts. No political truth is certainly of greater intrinsic value, or is stamped with the authority of more enlightened patrons of liberty, than that on which the objection is founded.

The accumulation of all powers, legislative, executive, and judiciary, in the same hands, whether of one, a few, or many, and whether hereditary, self appointed, or elective, may justly be pronounced the very definition of tyranny. Were the federal Constitution, therefore, really chargeable with the accumulation of power, or with a mixture of powers, having a dangerous tendency to such an accumulation, no further arguments would be necessary to inspire a universal reprobation of the system. I persuade myself, however, that it will be made apparent to every one, that the charge cannot be supported, and that the maxim on which it relies has been totally misconceived and misapplied. In order to form correct ideas on this important subject, it will be proper to investigate the sense in which the preservation of liberty requires that the three great departments of power should be separate and distinct. The oracle who is always consulted and cited on this subject is the celebrated Montesquieu. If he be not the author of this invaluable precept in the science of politics, he has the merit at least of displaying and recommending it most effectually to the attention of mankind. Let us endeavor, in the first place, to ascertain his meaning on this point. The British Constitution was to Montesquieu what Homer has been to the didactic writers on epic poetry. As the latter have considered the work of the immortal bard as the perfect model from which the principles and rules of the epic art were to be drawn, and by which all similar works were to be judged, so this great political critic appears to have viewed the Constitution of England as the standard, or to use his own expression, as the mirror of political liberty; and to have delivered, in the form of elementary truths, the several characteristic principles of that particular system. That we may be sure, then, not to mistake his meaning in this case, let us recur to the source from which the maxim was drawn. On the slightest view of the British Constitution, we must perceive that the legislative, executive, and judiciary departments are by no means totally separate and distinct from each other. The executive magistrate forms an integral part of the legislative authority. He alone has the prerogative of making treaties with foreign sovereigns, which, when made, have, under certain limitations, the force of legislative acts. All the members of the judiciary department are appointed by him, can be removed by him on the address of the two Houses of Parliament, and form, when he pleases to consult them, one of his constitutional councils. One branch of the legislative department forms also a great constitutional council to the executive chief, as, on another hand, it is the sole depositary of judicial power in cases of impeachment, and is invested with the supreme appellate jurisdiction in all other cases. The judges, again, are so far connected with the legislative department as often to attend and participate in its deliberations, though not admitted to a legislative vote . . . The magistrate in whom the whole executive power resides cannot of himself make a law, though he can put avnegative on every law; nor administer justice in person, though he has the appointment of those who do administer it. The judges can exercise no executive prerogative, though they are shoots from the executive stock; nor any legislative function, though they may be advised with by the legislative councils. The entire legislature can perform no judiciary act, though by the joint act of two of its branches the judges may be removed from their offices, and though one of its branches is possessed of the judicial power in the last resort. The entire legislature, again, can exercise no executive prerogative, though one of its branches constitutes the supreme executive magistracy, and another, on the impeachment of a third, can try and condemn all the subordinate officers in the executive department. The reasons on which Montesquieu grounds his maxim are a further demonstration of his meaning. ``When the legislative and executive powers are united in the same person or body," says he, ``there can be no liberty, because apprehensions may arise lest THE SAME monarch or senate should ENACT tyrannical laws to EXECUTE them in a tyrannical manner." Again: ``Were the power of judging joined with the legislative, the life and liberty of the subject would be exposed to arbitrary control, for THE JUDGE would then be THE LEGISLATOR . . ."

PUBLIUS.

Anti-Federalist Essay No. 47: "Balance" of Departments Not Achieved Under New Constitution

This essay is made up of excerpts from "Centinel's," letters of October 5 and 24, 1787. Taken from *The Independent Gazetteer*.

I am fearful that the principles of government inculcated in Mr. [John] Adams' treatise [Defence of the Constitutions of Government of the United States of America], and enforced in the numerous essays and paragraphs in the newspapers, have misled some well designing members of the late Convention. But it will appear in the sequel, that the construction of the proposed plan of government is infinitely more extravagant.

I have been anxiously expecting that some enlightened patriot would, ere this, have taken up the pen to expose the futility, and counteract the baneful tendency of such principles. Mr. Adams' sine qua non [Latin: "without which, not"] of a good government is three balancing powers; whose repelling qualities are to produce an equilibrium of interests, and thereby promote the happiness of the whole community. He asserts that the administrators of every government, will ever be actuated by views of private interest and ambition, to the prejudice of the public good; that therefore the only effectual method to secure the rights of the people and promote their welfare, is to create an opposition of interests between the members of two distinct bodies, in the exercise of the powers of government, and balanced by those of a third. This hypothesis supposes human wisdom competent to the task of instituting three co-equal orders in government, and a corresponding weight in the community to enable them respectively to exercise their several parts, and whose views and interests should be so distinct as to prevent a coalition of any two of them for the destruction of the third. Mr. Adams, although he has traced the constitution of every form of government that ever existed, as far as history affords materials, has not been able to adduce a single instance of such a government. He indeed says that the British constitution is such in theory, but this is rather a confirmation that his principles are chimerical and not to be reduced to practice. If such an organization of power were practicable, how long would it continue? Not a day—for there is so great a disparity in the talents, wisdom and industry of mankind, that the scale would presently preponderate to one or the other body, and with every accession of power the means of further increase would be greatly extended. The state of society in England is much more favorable to such a scheme of government than that of America. There they have a powerful hereditary nobility, and real distinctions of rank and interests; but even there, for want of that perfect equality of power and distinction of interests in the three orders of government, they exist but in name. The only operative and efficient check upon the conduct of administration, is the sense of the people at large.

Suppose a government could be formed and supported on such principles, would it answer the great purposes of civil society? If the administrators of every government are actuated by views of private interest and ambition, how is the welfare and happiness of the community to be the result of such jarring adverse interests?

Therefore, as different orders in government will not produce the good of the whole, we must recur to other principles. I believe it will be found that the form of government, which holds those entrusted with power in the greatest responsibility to their constituents, the best calculated for freemen. A republican, or free government, can only exist where the body of the people are virtuous, and where property is pretty equally divided. In such a government the people are the sovereign and their sense or opinion is the criterion of every public measure. For when this ceases to be the case, the nature of the government is changed, and an aristocracy, monarchy or despotism will rise on its ruin. The highest responsibility is to be attained in a simple structure of government, for the great body of the people never steadily attend to the operations of government, and for want of due information are liable to be imposed on. If you complicate the plan by various orders, the people will be perplexed and divided in their sentiment about the source of abuses or misconduct; some will impute it to the senate, others to the house of representatives, and so on, that the interposition of the people may be rendered imperfect or perhaps wholly abortive. But if, imitating the constitution of Pennsylvania, you vest all the legislative power in one body of men (separating the executive and judicial) elected for a short period, and necessarily excluded by rotation from permanency, and guarded from precipitancy and surprise by delays imposed on its proceedings, you will create the most perfect responsibility. For then, whenever the people feel a grievance, they cannot mistake the authors, and will apply the remedy with certainty and effect, discarding them at the next election. This tie of responsibility will obviate all the dangers apprehended from a single legislature, and will the best secure the rights of the people . . .

This mixture of the legislative and executive moreover highly tends to corruption. The chief improvement in government, in modern times, has been the complete separation of the great distinctions of power; placing the legislative in different hands from those which hold the executive; and again severing the judicial part from the ordinary administrative. "When the legislative and executive powers (says Montesquieu) are united in the same person or in the same body of magistrates, there can be no liberty."

CENTINEL

TIMELINE

1781   Articles of Confederation go into effect.

1786   A convention meets in Annapolis, Maryland, to discuss the Articles of Confederation.

1787   The Constitutional Convention is held. The Federalist and Anti-Federalist essays begin to appear in various newspapers. The Constitution is drafted and approved; it is ratified by Delaware, Pennsylvania, and New Jersey.

1788   Federalist and Anti-Federalist essays continue to be published. Eight more states agree to ratify the Constitution.

1789   The Constitution takes effect. North Carolina ratifies the Constitution.

1790   Rhode Island ratifies the Constitution.

1791   The Bill of Rights is added to the Constitution.

GLOSSARY

anarchy A state of lawlessness.

bicameral Having two chambers or houses.

faction An individual group that gathers for political or economic interests.

judicial Relating to courts of law or to the administration of justice.

legislation The act or process of legislating; lawmaking.

ordinance An authoritative command or order.

propaganda Material given out or published by the advocates or opponents of a doctrine or cause.

pseudonym A pen or pretend name used in publishing.

ratification The process of approving or agreeing to something officially.

treason A violation of allegiance or loyalty toward one's country, especially the betrayal of one's country by waging war against it or by consciously and purposely acting to help its enemies.

tyranny A government in which one person has all the power.

FOR MORE INFORMATION

The Constitution Society
7793 Burnet Road, #37
Austin, TX 78757
(512) 374-9585
Web site: http://www.constitution.org

World Federalist Association
418 Seventh Street SE
Washington, DC 20003
(800) 932-0123
Web site: http://www.wfa.org

Web Sites

Due to the changing nature of Internet links, the Rosen Publishing Group, Inc., has developed an online list of Web sites related to the subject of this book. This site is updated regularly. Please use this link to access the list:

http://www.rosenlinks.com/ghds/fado

FOR FURTHER READING

Collier, Christopher. *Building a New Nation: The Federalist Era: 1789–1801*. Salt Lake City: Benchmark Books, 1998.

Decarolis, Lisa. *Alexander Hamilton: Federalist and Founding Father*. New York: Powerkids Press, 2003.

Payan, Gregory. *The Federalists and Anti-Federalists: How and Why Political Parties Were Formed in Young America*. New York: Rosen Publishing Group, 2003.

BIBLIOGRAPHY

Elkins, Stanley, and Eric McKitrick. *The Age of Federalism*. New York: Oxford University Press, 1994.

Hakim, Joy. *The New Nation, 1789–1850*. New York: Oxford University Press, 2003.

Ketcham, Ralph, ed. *The Anti-Federalist Papers and the Constitutional Convention Debates*. New York: Signet, 2003.

Meisner, James Jr., and Amy Ruth. *American Revolutionaries and Founders of the Nation*. Springfield, NJ: Enslow Publishers, 1999.

Old, Wendie C. *Thomas Jefferson* (United States Presidents). Springfield, NJ: Enslow Publishers, 1997.

Rossiter, Clinton, ed. *The Federalist Papers*. New York: Mentor, 1999.

Whitelaw, Nancy. *More Perfect Union: The Story of Alexander Hamilton* (Notable Americans). Greensboro, NC: Morgan Reynolds, Inc., 1997.

PRIMARY SOURCE IMAGE LIST

Page 4 (left): Portrait of Alexander Hamilton, oil on canvas, circa 1790–1795. Courtesy of Independence National Historical Park in Philadelphia, Pennsylvania.

Page 4 (right): Portrait of Thomas Jefferson, 1791, oil on canvas by Charles Willson Peale. Housed at the Independence National Historical Park in Philadelphia Pennsylvania.

Page 10 (left): The Articles of Confederation, November 15, 1777. Housed at the National Archives in Washington, D.C.

Page 10 (right): Portrait of John Dickinson, 1780, by Charles W. Peale. Housed at Independence Hall in Philadelphia, Pennsylvania.

Page 11: The Northwest Ordinance, July 13, 1787. Housed at the National Archives in Washington, D.C.

Page 13: Illustration of Daniel Shays, 1787, published in *Bickerstaff's Boston Almanack*.

Page 15: *Convention at Philadelphia*, engraving, 1823. Artist unknown. Housed at the Library of Congress Prints and Photographs Division in Washington, D.C.

Page 19: John Jay, oil on canvas, 1794. Painted by Gilbert Stuart. Housed at the National Gallery of Art in Washington, D.C.

Page 21 (left): Portrait of James Madison, 1783, by Charles Willson Peale. Housed at the Library of Congress Rare Books and Special Collections Divisions in Washington, D.C.

Page 21 (right): A page of James Madison's notes of a debate in Congress on the creation of the Library of Congress, 1783. Housed at the Library of Congress Manuscript Division in Washington, D.C.

Page 23: Portrait of Richard Henry Lee, engraving by Johnson, Fry, and Co., circa 1860. Housed at the Library of Congress Prints and Photographs Division in Washington, D.C.

Page 29: Pages from *The New-York Packet*, November 20, 1787.

Page 33: *The Looking Glass for 1787*, satirical engraving by Amos Doolittle, 1787. Housed at the Library of Congress Prints and Photographs Division in Washington, D.C.

Page 36 (left): George Washington's copy of the Virginia Plan, 1787. Housed at the Library of Congress in Washington, D.C.

Page 36 (right): *First President*, undated engraving by Alonzo Chapel.

Page 38: May 28, 1788, issue of *The New-York Packet* that carried essay 74, written by Alexander Hamilton.

Page 40: Copy of the first edition of *The Federalist: A Collection of Essays, Written in Favour of the New Constitution*, 1788. Housed at the Library of Congress Rare Books and Special Collections Division in Washington, D.C.

Page 43 (right): July 7, 1793, letter from Thomas Jefferson to James Madison. Housed at the Library of Congress Manuscript Division in Washington, D.C.

Page 45: January 10, 1788 edition of the *New-York Journal, and Weekly Register*, carrying Brutus's eighth essay.

INDEX

A

amendments, 11, 46, 50
American Herald, 17
American Revolution, 5, 6
Anti-Federalist essays, 22–25, 44–46
Anti-Federalists, 5, 7, 16, 17, 21–24, 41, 42–49
Articles of Confederation, 6, 8–13, 14, 18, 26, 28, 31, 33, 35

B

bill of rights, 39, 44
Brutus 6, 22, 48–49
Bryan, Samuel, 22

C

Cato, 6, 22
Centinel, 22
checks and balances, system of, 14, 22, 35, 37, 39
Cincinnatus, 6, 22
Clinton, George, 22
Congress, 9, 10, 11, 46
Constitution, 7, 15–16, 17, 18, 20, 22, 26, 34, 35, 37–39, 41, 42, 43–44, 45, 46, 48, 49, 50
Constitutional Convention, 13–14, 18, 20

D

debate, 5–7, 17–18, 28, 41, 49
DeWitt, John, 44–45
Duer, William, 20

E

executive branch, 9

F

Federal Farmer, 22, 46–47
Federalist Papers, 18–21, 26–34, 36–41, 44

Federalists, 5–6, 7, 16, 17–18, 20–21, 24, 26, 31, 34, 35, 37, 38, 41, 42, 43, 44, 45, 46, 49
Freeman's Journal, 17

G

Grayson, William, 24
Great Britain/England, 6, 8, 18, 38, 44

H

Hamilton, Alexander, 7, 18, 20, 21, 26, 27, 28, 30–31, 33, 35, 38–39, 41
Henry, Patrick, 7, 24
House of Representatives, 14

I

Independent Journal, 16, 17, 22

J

Jay, John, 18–20, 26, 28, 41
Jefferson, Thomas, 7, 22, 42
judicial branch, 9, 37, 38

K

Knox, Henry, 11

L

Lee, Arthur, 22
Lee, Richard Henry, 22

M

Madison, James, 7, 20–21, 26, 30, 35, 37, 41
Morris, Gouverneur, 20

N

New Jersey Plan, 14
Northwest Ordinance, 10–11

P

Penn, William, 24

Poughkeepsie Country Journal, 17, 22, 46
pseudonyms/pen names, 5–6, 22–24, 44
Publius, 6, 20

R
Revolutionary War (American Revolution),
    5, 6, 8, 10, 12, 18, 42, 44

S
Senate, 14, 38
separation of powers, 35, 37, 39
Shays's Rebellion, 12
slavery, 10

Smith, Melancton, 22
Supreme Court, 14, 34

V
Virginia Plan, 14

W
Warren, Mercy, 24
Washington, George, 11, 13, 18, 20, 50

Y
Yates, Robert, 22

About the Author

Lea Ball is a full-time writer and author living in Portland, Oregon. She is the homeschooling mother to four children and life partner to Joseph. She has written more than three dozen nonfiction books for children, young adults, and families. She has a degree in secondary education and English from Ball State University and spends all of her time reading, talking, and staring at the Pacific Northwest scenery.

Photo Credits

Cover, pp. 10 (right), 23, Independence National Historic Park; pp. 9, 15, 21 (left), 29 (inset), 33, 43 (left) Library of Congress Prints and Photographs Division; pp. 10 (left), 11 National Archives and Records Administration; p. 19 The Supreme Court of the United States Office of the Curator; pp. 21 (right), 36 (left), 43 (right) Library of Congress Manuscript Division; pp. 24 © Bettmann/Corbis; pp. 29, Collection of The New York Historical Society; p. 31 © Francis G. Mayer/ Corbis; p. 36 (right) © Hulton/Archive/Getty Images; pp. 38, 45 General Research Division, The New York Public Library, Astor, Lenox and Tilden Foundations; p. 40 Library of Congress Rare Books and Special Collections Division; p. 47 © Art Resource.

Designer: Les Kanturek; Editor: Wayne Anderson